"It's Not My Fault"

MAN'S BIG MISTAKE

By Marilyn Lashbrook

Illustrated by Chris Sharp

ME TOO!

Fort Collins, Colorado

ME TOO! READERS are designed to help you share the joy of reading with children. They provide a new and fun way to improve a child's reading skills — by practice and example. At the same time, you are teaching your child valuable Bible truths.

"IT'S NOT MY FAULT" helps children understand the importance of making right choices. This fascinating story gives you the opportunity to discuss: resisting temptation, accepting the consequences, shifting the blame and receiving forgiveness.

Reading is the key to successful education. Obeying the principles of God's Word opens the door to a successful life. ME TOO! READERS encourage your children in both!

Bold type:	Child reads
Regular type:	Adult reads
● :	Wait for child to respond
♥♥ :	Talk about it!

Library of Congress Catalog Card Number: 90- 60459
ISBN 0-86606-439-7

Art direction and design by
    Chris Schechner Graphic Design

"It's Not My Fault"

MAN'S BIG MISTAKE

By Marilyn Lashbrook

Illustrated by Chris Sharp

Taken from Genesis 3

ME TOO!
R E A D E R S

Long ago, when the world was brand new, God made the very first man. Adam lived in a magnificent garden. He cared for the plants, trained the animals, and best of all, he visited with God.

There was only one rule for Adam to obey. It was a simple one. Or so it seemed.

"You may eat as much fruit as you like," said God. "You may eat from any tree you like . . . except the Tree of the Knowledge of Good and Evil.

"Do not eat from that tree!" God said, "If you do, you will die."

It didn't seem like a hard rule to obey. But it was not as easy as it sounded.

Adam could eat juicy red apples and sweet bananas. He could eat peaches and pears and persimmons. He could even eat from the Tree of Life. It was his choice.

But if he made the wrong choice - if he broke God's rule - he would bring death into the wonderful world God had made.

The garden was a great place to live. Adam had an important job to do, too. But sometimes, he was lonely.

To cheer him up, God brought all the animals to Adam. God told Adam to think of names for them. Adam named the mischievous monkeys. He named the howling hyena. He named the enormous elephant. What fun it was to choose just the right name for each one.

If you had been the first person on earth, what would you have named the animals on this page? ⬣

Adam enjoyed naming animals, smelling flowers, and tasting luscious fruit. He especially enjoyed his time with God. But Adam was still lonely, for he was the only man on earth.

**"It is not good for man to be alone,"
God said. So God made a woman and
brought her to Adam. Eve would be Adam's
friend and helper. She would be his wife.**

**Adam was very happy. Now he had
everything he needed.**

**But just when things seemed perfect,
along came . . .**

the serpent.

He was sly and sneaky — the sneakiest
of all animals.

The serpent was God's enemy. He
wanted to hurt God.

He knew God loved Adam and Eve. So
the serpent decided to trick them into
disobeying. That would hurt God more
than anything.

First, the serpent tried to make God's rule seem unfair. "Did God really tell you not to eat from any fruit tree in the garden?" he asked.

Eve thought a minute. "No," she said, "but we can't even touch the tree in the middle of the garden. If we do, we will die!"

That wasn't true. God only told them not to eat the fruit.

So the sleazy, slippery, slimy old serpent tried to make God look like a liar. "You won't really die!" said the serpent with a snicker. ●

"God knows you will be like Him if you eat the fruit. You will be wise and you will know good and evil."

Well, that did it! Eve believed the serpent. She wanted to be like God. And the fruit looked so pretty. It would surely taste delicious!

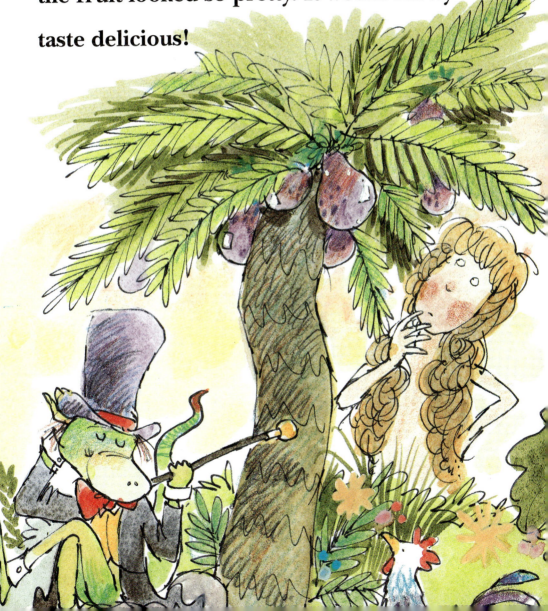

So Eve picked some. She took a bite.
Then she gave some to Adam.

Now Adam had a hard choice to make.
He knew it was wrong to eat the fruit, but
Eve wanted him to taste some. Adam
listened to his wife. He took the fruit and
ate it. That was a BIG mistake.

Suddenly, Adam and Eve felt very
different inside. They felt guilty and
ashamed.

They felt different on the outside too.
All at once, they saw they needed clothes.

Adam and Eve sewed fig leaves together
to make clothes for themselves.

The garden was cool and comfortable and the sound of chirping birds was peaceful, but Adam and his wife had no peace. They were terrified of facing God. They worried about what would happen to them.

When they heard God walking in the garden, they hid from Him.

"Where are you?" God called.

Adam answered, "I heard you coming. I was afraid. I am naked, so I hid."

"Have you eaten the fruit?" God asked. God knew the answer, but He wanted Adam to tell what he had done.

Adam did not want to admit he was wrong. He wanted to blame someone else. "It's not MY fault!" Adam exclaimed, "the woman YOU made gave me the fruit."

God looked at the woman. "What have you done?"

The woman did not want to take the blame either. "It's not MY fault!" Eve argued. "It was the SERPENT. HE tricked me into eating the fruit."

The serpent said nothing. He just SMIRKED!

So God said to the serpent, "Because you did this, you will crawl on your belly and eat dust all the days of your life."

That was not all. Eve would have children. And they would have children. And their children would have children. And one day, one of their children would give birth to Jesus, God's Son.

The serpent would try to kill Jesus, but Jesus would live again.

And one day, God's Son would destroy the serpent and all of his followers.

Even though the serpent tricked Eve, she had made her own choice. It was the wrong choice. She must be punished too.

"It will be very painful to have babies," God said to Eve, "and from now on, your husband will rule over you."

Adam made a choice too. He had chosen to disobey God.

"The ground is cursed because of your sin," God said. Then God told him it would take hard, sweaty work to grow vegetables to eat. Wooly worms and weeds would damage Adam's crops.

But worst of all, Adam and his wife, and all people after them would grow old and die.

God still loved Adam and Eve, though.

He made fur coats for them to wear.

But nothing would ever be the same. Adam and Eve would have to move out of the beautiful garden. Walks and talks with God would be very different now. Life would be full of struggles, for sin always brings pain and sorrow.

But Adam and Eve were not without hope. Someday, Jesus would come. He would wash away their sin and bring forgiveness to all people.

Adam and Eve had another choice to make. The choice to believe God. And they did!

You have choices too. What will you choose to do? 🖤🖤

ME TOO!
B O O K S

For Ages 2-5

SOMEONE TO LOVE
THE STORY OF CREATION

TWO BY TWO
THE STORY OF NOAH'S FAITH

"I DON'T WANT TO"
THE STORY OF JONAH

"I MAY BE LITTLE"
THE STORY OF DAVID'S GROWTH

"I'LL PRAY ANYWAY"
THE STORY OF DANIEL

WHO NEEDS A BOAT?
THE STORY OF MOSES

"GET LOST LITTLE BROTHER"
THE STORY OF JOSEPH

THE WALL THAT DID NOT FALL
THE STORY OF RAHAB'S FAITH

NO TREE FOR CHRISTMAS
THE STORY OF JESUS' BIRTH

"NOW I SEE"
THE STORY OF THE MAN BORN BLIND

DON'T ROCK THE BOAT!
THE STORY OF THE MIRACULOUS CATCH

OUT ON A LIMB
THE STORY OF ZACCHAEUS

SOWING AND GROWING
THE PARABLE OF THE SOWER AND THE SOILS

DON'T STOP . . . FILL EVERY POT
THE STORY OF THE WIDOW'S OIL

GOOD, BETTER, BEST
THE STORY OF MARY AND MARTHA

GOD'S HAPPY HELPERS
THE STORY OF TABITHA AND FRIENDS

ME TOO!
R E A D E R S

For Ages 5-8

IT'S NOT MY FAULT
MAN'S BIG MISTAKE

GOD, PLEASE SEND FIRE!
ELIJAH AND THE PROPHETS OF BAAL

TOO BAD, AHAB!
NABOTH'S VINEYARD

THE WEAK STRONGMAN
SAMSON

NOTHING TO FEAR
JESUS WALKS ON WATER

THE BEST DAY EVER
THE STORY OF JESUS

THE GREAT SHAKE-UP
MIRACLES IN PHILIPPI

TWO LADS AND A DAD
THE PRODIGAL SON

Available at your local bookstore or from:

Treasure!

MSC 1000   829 S. Shields
Fort Collins, CO 80521
1-800-284-0158